Tl

Harnessing the Power of Words, Symbols, and Imagery for a Happy, Healthy, & Successful Life

By Dario Thomas: copyright 12/31/15

The Way of the Warlock

Table of Contents

Pg10 :Chapter 1: Warlock Facts and Fictions

Pg36 :Chapter 2: The Power of Words

The Way of the Warlock

Pg67 :Chapter 3: Invocations, Incantations, Rituals, Spells, and Symbols

Pg128: Chapter 4: How to Make and Use a Magic Wand

Pg 136: Chapter 5: Lucidity the Clear Mind

Disclaimer

The author of this manuscript does not claim to be a magician, wizard, or stereotypical warlock. This book is not meant to encourage the reader to indulge in occult practices or to try and gain unfair advantages or control over others. This book does give a brief synopsis of witches and witchcraft. It depicts the ways and practices of the stereotypical wicked witch of "old;" the author does acknowledge that many modern day witches have shed this common viewpoint of witchery and are practicing their crafts for benevolent purposes. This book is not intended to promote or demote the use of witchcraft in any way, shape, or form. Most importantly, this book is not intended to be a substitute for medical or psychological help and treatment. If you are under the care of a doctor for medical or psychological reasons, the author does not endorse ceasing to get treatments because of the reading of this material; if you suspect that you may have any mental or physical ailments, then again, this book is not to be considered a valid source of professional help.

The Way of the Warlock

Preface

You are now about to embark on a wonderfully magnificent life changing journey. You are about to learn the way of the warlock. Right about now, many preconceived notions are probably swimming through your head; however, the author asks that you temporarily suspend those viewpoints (at least until you finish reading this book). The veil of superstition will be rent. You will breathe a sigh of relief as the truth floods your mental household with light because the light will chase away all falsity and nonsense. The light will disperse the darkness, leaving you with a sense of peace and total bliss. You will be able to navigate your life's journey with a level of faith and stress free attitudes beyond your wildest dreams as things miraculously flow according to your will. Read the book once from cover to cover. Next go back and study it; practice the techniques. Keep in mind that practice makes perfect. Just like building physical structures, mental and spiritual mansions can be built likewise (it's all a process but it doesn't happen overnight); but it can be done and this book means to show you the way: the way of the warlock.

The Way of the Warlock

Introduction

We are here. And that is pretty much the gist of it. We are here and that is all we know. We don't know why we are here, but nevertheless, we are here. Another thing is this. People come and people go. We form relationships for a period of time and then we either go our separate ways or break the bonds. Many of our friends, loved ones, and even enemies have passed on from this earthly realm, much to our sorrow or relief. Yet and still we do not know why. Enter the invention of religion. That's right; I said "invention." God did not create religion. Man did. Why? Because man needed to know and understand why we are here: why we come and why we go. Interestingly enough, religion has failed to give man the answers that he so desperately seeks. But religion has done the very opposite; it (with the help of the undercover warlocks) has cast a massive eerily strange sort of hypnotic spell over its congregations that eventually spewed over to affect the entire planet. By way of organized religion, man has been thrown into spiritual abysses and mental labyrinths. He believes himself to be headed toward the light but he recoils in fear. It is a satanic spell and man now thinks that the darkness is his salvation. This is where this book comes into play: it shows the way to true spiritual freedom and success.

The Way of the Warlock

Chapter 1: Warlock Facts and Fictions

Organized Religion Debunked

Being a warlock is something (a practice if you will) that organized religion (especially organized Christianity) writes off as being taboo. It is a lifestyle that supposedly (according to religion) serves to dedicate the life of the practicer to the devil. What's worse is that (according to religion) this sort of practice is considered sorcery. Sorcery has been condemned in the bible as a devilish thing. The ironic thing about it all is this; even if you consider practicing real sorcery or witchcraft as taboo, in the hierarchy of taboos, both witchcraft and sorcery are in the lower to midlevel ranks. These are only intermediate taboos. The ultimate of all taboos is in fact not only practiced but it is blatantly encouraged by organized Christianity. You, the reader, may in fact be guilty of this diabolical practice. Therefore, the whole scope of organized religion, including organized Christianity, is a worldwide and perhaps the most evil and sorriest of all scams. Even Christ

Himself rebuked organized religion. You will learn why very soon.

The Way of the Warlock

What is life all about? (Excerpt from the book of Spiritology)

What is life all about? That is the ultimate question. Here is the answer. Although this may seem like a cop out reply, ultimately it is the only answer that can be given. The answer is this: forget about that question and never ever ask it again. This question can not only be answered from your limited (finite) point of view, but if the answer could be given to you, your finite point of physical, mental, and even spiritual space couldn't contain it all. You'd disintegrate; your entire system would explode on all three levels. Life in its entirety is the full unlimited and unfathomable presence of God Himself. Your individual mindset and consciousness cannot contain the entire presence and mind of God. It is impossible to do so; trying to fully understand Life (God) is a very dangerous thing to do. This is what (organized) religion has done, and this is why it has severely erred. Organized religion (especially organized Christianity) has brained washed countless masses of people and destroyed their lives as a result of this falsely "implied" claim. Even Christ

The Way of the Warlock

Himself never claimed to fully know it all. Organized religion has committed the ultimate of all taboos. As matter of fact it is the absolute worst of all spiritual taboos. To ask what Life is all about is to ask what God is all about. The answer cannot fully be known to one person and asking it has driven many people insane.

The Ultimate Taboo

"I know the Lord." That's it! The statement, "I know the Lord," is the first of all religious taboos that paves the way to all the others. As said earlier, "Organized religion (especially organized Christianity) has brained washed countless masses of people and destroyed their lives as a result of this falsely 'implied' claim." The implication is this: to know the Lord is to know Him completely. This implies that Life itself is fully understood. To falsely believe that you fully understand Life or know the Lord is to install a (God complex) mindset into your psychic system. The individual becomes spiritually blind and as a result, a demon is conjured up to dwell within his psyche. As you recall, your mental space being a "finite" vessel cannot contain God in His entirety. So what it does (to accommodate or contain the belief) is to shrink it to the size of your mind's capacity so that it can be contained, giving the believer an imaginary concept of God instead. This imaginary concept transmutes itself into an egotistical notion that he himself is a god, and a demon is born. The disastrous result is everything (all sin, error, and fallacies) that you and everyone else know that are common everyday practices of the church. The individual now believes that he is guided by the Lord when in fact he is driven by the devil. He is now compelled to act out that God complex by way of organizing, controlling, and taking advantage of others. For those that don't develop a God complex, the true God (and Christ the Light) is reduced to something like a "childhood" imaginary friend. They then go around telling people that they know, talk to, and commune with God and Jesus, when in fact it is the devil deceiving them and causing them to fall deeper and deeper into spiritual darkness. This is a grave error, and the sad thing is this: there is not a single sect of organized religion that hasn't committed this sin of all sins. Indeed the ultimate taboo is (ironically) promoted and perpetrated by the organized religious factions. The average Christian is a child of the devil. This is why Christ Himself said,

"You are of your father, the devil, and it is your will to practice the lusts and gratify the desires [which are characteristic] of your father. He was a murderer from the beginning and does not stand in truth, because there is no truth in him. When he speaks a falsehood, he speaks what is natural to him, for he is a liar [himself] and the father of lies and of all that is false."

This verse is from the book of John, 8:44 - Amplified Bible.

They are lying to themselves and lying to each other. This is the original lie that leads to all other lies and sins that are (if sin can really be ranked) much worse than sorcery and witchcraft: for starters, how about the brutal murders (in the name of religion) and violating of innocent children. The brainwashed masses cannot understand what's happened to them simply because they've been brainwashed. But all is not lost; a brainwashed individual can be brain-cleansed.

The Better Question

As said previously said, the catch 22 question about life cannot be answered and should not attempt to be answered. However, that seems to leave the individual in a scary and confusing predicament. We still want to understand why we are here and where will we go after we depart from this earth. So a better question is in order. Here is that question,

"What is my personal life supposed to be about?"

Although, your individual mindset and consciousness cannot contain the entire presence and mind of God and the entirety of His unlimited knowledge, your system can contain each and every answer (given to you by the Higher Power) that you could think to ask (with regard to your personal life). You will be shown how to get the answers to all of your questions pertaining to your individualized life.

You cannot know God

You cannot know God, but you can connect to Him. You can totally surrender (internally) to God thereby allowing Him to give to you what you now believe yourself to be getting from God, but in actuality are receiving from the devil. What do you think you are getting from God but (in truth) are receiving from the devil? For starters, how about truth, guidance, and understanding. If you were actually connecting to God, there'd be no room in your mind for fear, confusion, or frustration.

"I and the Father are One."

Christ (the Light) uttered this statement quite often. What was he saying? Simply put, He was saying I am connected to God the Father (the Source of all things seen and unseen). This too can be your lot. It is with direct connection to God that you can get an answer to any question that you could ever think to ask for your individualized life. You will also be shown the way of true connection.

What exactly is a Warlock?

Historically speaking, traditional viewpoints of the warlock have had much negative connotation. Even now as you read the title of this manuscript, your imagination probably forged an image in your head: the image being that of a male witch. The interesting thing about it (from the author's personal perspective) is that it's kind of hard to formulate a picture of a male witch. When you mention the word witch, an image of a woman usually comes to mind. It reminds me of the term "nurse." Although there are male nurses, whenever the word is mentioned, an image of a female in a white uniform or scrubs comes to mind. A witch is a witch. The image (of a decrepit older woman) is deeply engrained in the psyche of many, but when you add to it the word "male," you have to step outside of the box and think to yourself, "What does a male witch even look like?" He really doesn't have any traditionally assigned attire like a witch's black dress, pointed hat, and broom. Neither have you heard of any flying around on these brooms with black cats in tow. Even the Halloween holiday shows little or no mention of the warlock. You have to make an effort to call up the image. Throughout history, when it comes to witches versus warlocks, witches are the most dominant throughout the times. Warlocks only have an "honorable mention" at best. There is a reason for this, and a much sinister reason it is. That reason will be soon revealed. Since warlocks haven't had much publicity over the centuries, perhaps the best way to drive home a better idea of them and what they were supposed to be about (from the stereotypical viewpoint) would be to give to you (per the author's best understanding)…

The Way of the Witch

From the stereotypical viewpoint, a witch is of the female gender. A witch is said to have openly renounced God and overtly dedicated herself, her life's purpose (soul and existence) to the devil in the "here and now" and in the "hereafter." Basically, a witch has agreed to go to hell in exchange for (earthly) power, longevity, and certain forms of human control and other benefits. A witch is somewhat like a sales representative for the devil. They sell insurance policies that must be (figuratively speaking and sometimes literally) signed with blood that have "fine print" written in invisible ink that the client is never made aware of. In other words you don't know what you are getting into when you consult a witch for help, but you can rest assured that it's always a bad deal. Also, the policy always has to be periodically renewed. Witches practice what's called "black magic." In theory, "black magic" is a mind over matter force (a power fortified by negative energy) that is said to be able to move "heaven and earth" to grant an individual whatever he wishes. It has been said that "black magic" can override even those that profess to have faith in God which is why many Christians (still to this day) seek the help of witches and their counterparts (mediums and psychics).

Seeking to consult the dead violates to law of God. Like Lot's wife (who was warned along with everyone else) not to look back as they exited Sodom and Gomorrah, the dead cannot turn back; if they could then their souls would truly be damned just like Lot's unfortunate wife. The dead are to move on to the next phase of existence; God has set up the law to work this way, and no one has the authority to violate it. In theory, a medium or witch (if they are not fraudulent) can rummage through your memory banks because you are nervously receptive (mentally wide open) and they can tell you what you want to hear; otherwise you get put into a sort of trance and a demon speaks on behalf of the dead loved one.

Human nature is designed to seek after immediate gratification and witchcraft (black magic) is supposed to be able to deliver. What makes it evil is that seeking the help of witches ultimately equates to making a deal with the devil. When witches help others, there is always a hidden agenda that most do not know about. Their ultimate aim is to prolong their very own lives by absorbing the spiritual essence of their clients (even to the point of death) by tricking them into forming unhealthy attachments. Here is an example:

If you suffer from arthritis in your knee and seek a witch for help and healing, she'd cast a spell to remove the infirmity, but the ailment, although removed from the knee, doesn't really go away. Instead, it gets suppressed. The pain may go away, but the ill condition remains. Because of the suppression, the client mistakes it for healing. The ailment might even start to fester (get worse) because the client may have foolishly stopped medical treatment (often times because of the ill advice of the witch). At some point much later on down the road, the pain returns. The pain is much worse. If the knee doesn't present any more problems, then the negative energy that supported the diseased area moves to another part of the body. Therefore a completely different ailment eventually pops up as a result. The individual is compelled to seek the witch's help again. This scenario eventually develops into a pattern in the life of the client. He at some point becomes totally dependent upon the witch. Other spells, like love spells and money spells tend to work and backfire in the same fashion. For instance if a love spell is cast on an individual against their will, the black magic being a negative energy source is (in theory) infused into the victim of the love spell's mind by way of telepathy or thought transference. The victim falls "head over heels" for the client; however, by way of the negative energy, the relationship quickly turns rocky, unbearable, and even volatile. Something inevitably (very major) will go wrong. The victim of the love spell may grow progressively evil, and if the client attempts to break it off, it may get ugly. Stalking and deadly violence can be the final result. The client is forced to continuously go to the witch for spells to correct each and every problem, and so it goes with money spells. The gained income by way of the negative energy

The Way of the Warlock

also attracts all sorts of mishaps and debt that the money has to be used for which keeps the client "behind the gun" financially speaking and consistently needing the witch as a system of support.

Over time the client is transformed into a helpless and depressed soul. He has in fact become addicted to the witch and dependent on black magic to make his life work. God is now out of the picture and the devil enters to claim him. But again, the remedies are only temporary, and as the individual gets sicker and sicker in both mind and body, this equates to and is how the witch gradually saps his very life's force from him absorbing the clients spiritual essence into her very own (mental and physical) vessel to selfishly and deviously preserve her own earthly existence. Although he may be traveling in the slow lane, the client is on his way to hell. It is by way of witchcraft or black magic that the devil is said to collect souls. The witch's power tends to grow in this fashion. If the client figures out what's really going on and tries to break away from the witch's influence, it may be easier for him if he was involved with the mafia and attempted to quit. The witch, being a witch, turns on the client and uses black magic to either keep him under her wing or curse him outright all together.

The witch however, doesn't get off scot-free. Absorbing second-hand life force into her physical vessel (as opposed to getting it directly from God) doesn't come with out a high price to pay. The second hand (warped) spiritual essence enters her mind and physique in a twisted (demented) state. Her body, although preserved, tends to become sickly and decrepit. Her mindset tends to become more evil, wicked, and conniving which causes her to greedily seek after more clients to drain. This is the reason why (traditionally) witches have been depicted as toothless, hump-backed, and decrepit old women with green skin. The absorbed essence of other human beings is like a drug addiction that gradually destroys her as well as her clients. Eventually, she herself succumbs to her very own addiction and she is finally indoctrinated into the kingdom of hell. Witches can only prolong their very own lives by

tricking others into being ensnared by
the devil.

Many do not realize that by being
dedicated to the devil, a witch cannot
truly heal. Only God is capable of true
healing. Healing is a virtue. Satan has
no virtue. Since the devil is void of
virtue, there is no way he can be
capable of true healing. He'd be turning
against himself. As Christ once said,
"How can satan cast out satan?" The
devil is incapable of doing the work of
the Lord, but he can fake it: and quite
convincingly too. Thus is the way of the
witch. Translate this depiction to the
male species and perhaps you have the
stereotypical warlock. Have you ever
heard of a wicked old warlock? I would
venture to say "no," but the cliché,
"wicked old witch" does resound quite
loudly in your mind's inner ear. Here is
the reason.

Stereotypical Warlocks Operate Underground

The way of the witch is not the way of the warlock; even in the stereotypical fashion, the warlock has not operated (practiced his craft) like the witch. The warlock has been much undercover throughout the centuries. They have hidden in the very place most have least expected. Where have they been hiding? First of all, let's review the ways of the witch:

Witches find clients, cast spells on their behalf, the spells don't quite work out as the client expects, repeat business leads to more spells being cast, they foster a sense of dependency upon themselves, the clients become addicted, they waste away until total (spiritual) depletion.

Ok, now to answer the question, where have the warlocks been hiding? They've been cleverly concealed within the ranks of the church. It is the author's personal opinion that the clergymen themselves are in fact warlocks. Just compare what they do to what witches do. They attract members to the church. They supposedly "save" their souls by way of prayers and confessions: this is pretty similar to witches casting spells because the clergy also uses rituals and incantations. They foster dependency by calling it fellowship with God. The congregations gradually grow addicted and develop attachments to the warlocks and the church organizations; all the while they fail to realize what true faith in God is all about. Their lives, just like the clients of witches, gradually go downhill (spiritually) as they become ensnared within mental prisons; trials and tribulations are all they know accompanied by brief interludes of elation, and they continuously seek the help of these warlocks to help themselves become free, but it is all in vain. These warlocks are all the popes, bishops, ministers, and pastors. That being said, there are even some female warlocks out there in this day and age. Some of the modern day warlocks appear in the form of the filthy rich mega church evangelists. They cast hypnotic spells over thousands at a time. They put them in trances and tell them that the "Holy Spirit" is upon them. These warlocks are very clever and crafty in that they steal souls almost immediately.

The Way of the Warlock

If you call them warlocks they will fiercely deny it. If you tell anyone in their congregations, that they are under the hypnotic spell of a warlock, they will severely rebuke you and tell you that he is a "man of God." To control others by fostering a mindset of "the devil will eventually have your soul if you do not conform to my way of thinking" is a blatant form of sorcery. It is a hypnotic spell that many fall into and fail to rise out of. And they end up in hell (the devil's bosom) anyway. I once dated a girl who had an unruly 5 year old boy. One day we were watching a horror movie. Personally, at the time, I was somewhat immature, but I did ask her, "Are you going to let him watch this?" She responded that he'd be ok. The kid sat there perfectly still, attentive, and wide eyed as the movie played. It clearly had an impact on him. Afterwards, whenever he tended to act out, I'd tell him that I was going to open the closet door and let the monster out later that night. As a result, he was quite obedient every time I came around. Whether you think this is bad or good, the fact is that this is exactly what the church and its undercover warlocks have done to its congregations.

The Way of the Warlock

The Witch Hunts

Not so long ago, society experienced a very dark era that was marked by "witch hunts." Women were falsely accused of practicing witchcraft and forced to confess (often times by physical torture). Many were dragged out of their homes, beaten mercilessly, and even burned alive. The people did it to drive the devil out from among themselves. Little or no proof was required. If there was a particular woman that you didn't like, all you had to do was tell the right person that she was a witch. That would pretty much be the end of her life, even if she was innocent. It is a no-brainer that many vindictive people did just that. They bore false witness against their neighbors; many (especially the cruel hypocritical undercover warlocks) did it for the sake of twisted indignant self righteous pleasure: much like a power tripping rapist gets pleasure over violating and abusing a woman. An innocent life would be destroyed and all the while satan remained among them to eventually call out and claim more innocent victims. But the plot thickens as the next segment will reveal.

The Way of the Warlock

Hypocrisy in High Places

Have you not noticed anything peculiar about the previous segment on "witch hunts?" The witch hunt was the gist of it all. There wasn't any mention of warlock hunts. Want to know why? Because the clergy (being warlocks that condemned the women as witches) was mostly run by men.

The clergy (church itself) became "satan the accuser" while simultaneously practicing secretly behind closed doors the black arts or even going to some of the witches to seek guidance and get spells cast on their behalf. Yes, it is a common case of "hypocrisy in high places." They often practiced in private what they condemned in public. The women that they accused were simply scapegoats to keep others from finding out the truth of the matter. When it comes to the modern day warlocks, the author believes that the practice of magic or even sorcery is the reason why they gained such massive and loyal followers (more like minions, if you will). After all, a form of sorcery is to put an individual in a trance to the point that he cannot even guard his own mind.

The Way of the Warlock

Afterwards, you proceed to populate his unguarded mind with anything you'd like him to believe. By instilling a belief in someone's mind (even if it's destructive) that person becomes a willing and obedient mental slave. This is how small children are ensnared. Their minds are very much unguarded and they tend to believe whatever is told to them. Has organized religion not done this for centuries already? Again, the witches were the sacrificial lambs being condemned by the warlocks to throw the church congregations off their very own devilish scents. The fear that resulted also served to keep the people obediently in line with their tyrannical rules and regulations.

The Man of God

Truly a real "man of God" wouldn't deceive people and hand them over to the devil so relentlessly. Therefore, since the clergy rejects the title of what they really are and refuse to acknowledge that they truly serve the devil, the author has decided to revamp the title of "Warlock" to a much nobler philosophy and way of life. We will say that a warlock is a true man of God. A warlock is a man that has rejected organized Christianity in order to embrace Christ Himself. A warlock is man that has real power to heal and edify. Some of the things he does seem to bear a striking resemblance to magic because of his faith in God. After all, when Christ turned water into wine, I suspect that many who didn't fully understand what was happening may have thought it was sorcery. Nevertheless, the magic (that the bible terms as miracles) was orchestrated by faith and faith alone. So a true warlock is a man that wields unlimited miracle producing spiritual power because of his unwavering faith in God.

The Way of the Warlock

The Warlock's Goal

A warlock's goal is the same as any other man of God's. He wants to ascend to the heavenly heights. He wants complete union and incessant communion with the source of all things seen and unseen: that is God the Father of Christ the Light. He wants to be Christlike. He wants to have that peace that passeth all understanding. He wants to understand beyond the intellect what it means to have a spirit of love and a sound mind. Basically he wants what you and everybody else wants: mental freedom and spiritual awakening.

Chapter 2: The Power of Words

The Source of Power

Words can be a source of tremendous power. Every day all day you see the power of words in action. Parents use words to direct and influence their children. A military officer uses words to command troops. A coach uses words to inspire athletes. A counselor uses words to advise and comfort people. Finally, interestingly enough, the previous usages of words are only part of the story. In the above examples the very same people can do the exact opposite with words. A parent can belittle and misguide a child; a military officer can sabotage his troops; a coach can humiliate an athlete; a counselor can cause a client to lose hope; all of this is possible with the usage of words. It is because of words that people are brainwashed and have lost their minds. They have been told lies (by way of words) about themselves and life in general, and the rest is history.

People are going bananas (losing faith) because of negative images swimming around inside their minds. These negative images are all because of (were initially jumpstarted by) wicked and wretched words that they either heard from others or told to themselves. The internal diabolical dialogues and malevolent monologues are gradually robbing (depleting) them of their very spiritual essences. Most of them have no clue that they can withdraw those words and use other (benevolent) words to deprive the inner demons of power to torment them any longer. For those that believe it is possible, they simply do not know how to accomplish it. The way of the warlock is the methodology.

The Way of the Warlock

Why do words contain so much power?

People are either rising or falling (mentally, physically, and spiritually) because of words. Right this moment, you the reader, are either going through gradual processes of self elevation or headed for self destruction. There is no standing still in the process of life. Life is always on the move. Your predominant mental state can clue you in on which direction you are headed in. If you don't have that same delightful sense of well being and cheeriness you once had as a child, then you have been misapplying your words and could be headed in the wrong direction. The power of words can literally change your life for the better practically overnight. They can practically give back to you that sense of well being, delight, and cheerful state you had as a child. If you use words correctly and properly apply them, your words can accomplish the following:

Give you a mind that is virtually fearless (not to be confused with gung-ho arrogant foolishness)

Bring you riches and wealth (more than you could ever hope to spend in your lifetime.

Correct and erase past errors [not repeating the same mistakes over and over again by releasing bad and negative attitudes].

Give you robust vigorous health, vitality, and unlimited energy.

Bring to you true love and healthy relationships

Cast away demons that vex you and employ angels to minister to you

Give you a true (real) conscious relationship with the Creator of all things seen and unseen beyond your current imaginary relationship.

Words have so much power because people invest emotional energy into them. The emotion is commonly known as belief or certainty. If you are certain that a particular word or phrase (of multiple words) has the power to accomplish whatever the symbolic meaning they are supposed to

The Way of the Warlock

represent, then they will do just that. Words are the instructions that tell the energy of emotion exactly what to do or create with them. The emotion combined with the words form a miniature angel that goes out into the ethers and does whatever the words command it to do. I've heard that in other cultures the words are said to create and release a genie; however, the effects are still the same. The previous list of seven items that tells what words can do for you is only the "tip of the iceberg." You can most certainly add to that list anything else that your mind can possibly conceive. It can be so. The author of this manuscript is willing to wager that even as were reading the list, a sense of hope and optimism for the future began to stir up inside of you. Your thought of the possibilities (using mentally induced words) to envision the things mentioned began to petition God and call up an angel to work on your behalf. Your true sense of natural happiness that the world has talked you into burying underneath all that negativity began to rumble (shake itself awake). That was your true spiritual essence crying out for freedom by being reminded that it once was free and can be free again. Such is the miracle working "power of words." You must learn to master words instead of allowing words to manipulate, control, and bind you.

The way of the warlock can make you a "master of words," hence you become a master of life.

Here is more icing on the cake or salt in the lemonade depending upon how you look at it. Do you realize that the influence of words extend far beyond the realm of human affairs? You may think you do, but if your life isn't unfolding as such (in the exact way that you want it to) then you do not. Keep the following spiritual law in mind at all times:

The Way of the Warlock

"**Realization equals implementation**."

It means that your true understanding or realization is what's actually happening in the real world for you (in your mind, body, and worldly affairs) at this very moment. There is such a thing as real realization and imaginary realization.

It's like a person that's never learned to swim. He sees others swimming every day. He then believes in the possibility of swimming; he even knows that swimming is possible based upon factual evidence (because he has seen it done). He mistakes this kind of knowing for "realization." It's called "intellectual knowing." He therefore thinks that he can swim. He even goes and wades in the shallow waters unscathed. Now he really thinks that he knows how to swim; after all, he has had experience of being in the waters; ay? He even tells others that he can swim. One day, he goes and jumps into the deep waters (over his head) and he drowns. Why? He had an imaginary realization of swimming as opposed to the real thing. He had intellectual knowing as opposed to true realization because he never really learned how to swim. True realization is the way of the warlock and you will be taught exactly how to rise above "intellectual knowing" to the realm of "true realization." You will be learning to use your words in the exact same way that God does. You will learn exactly why Christ Himself wielded so much power, and eventually true realization will be your reality.

Intellectual Knowing verses Walking in Faith

Take the word, "Faith." Right now, the word is dormant in the inner most recesses of your subconscious. Therefore, it remains an idle concept for you; however the truth of the matter is this. It is a word that (potentially) contains immense power (it can literally allow you to move heaven and earth) if you applied the word correctly; starting first with your mindset. When it comes to words, you have used your words to render yourself powerless and helpless by fostering the concept of "intellectual knowing" and erroneously substituting it for realization. You have imaginary knowing as opposed to real knowing. When it comes to faith, if you struggle and your walk isn't an automatic victorious process, then you are still in the infancy stage; however, the process does begin with intellectual knowing. That's how you get it into your head that certain things are possible. Intellectual knowing is the beginning (the planting of a seed). Afterwards, the seed must be cultivated (in fertile mental ground), nurtured, and allowed to grow, thereby eventually rising up out of unconscious intellectual knowing and into dynamic active conscious realization. Here is an example of "walking in faith."

I can vividly recall when one of my beloved nieces was a toddler. She was fumbling around, stumbling, and falling. She used various pieces of furniture to pull herself up and travel around the room. At the time, I and my mom were the only ones at home with her. I laughed and played with her for a brief moment; then I said to her, "Hey, you wanna go outside?" She smiled and nodded her head. I picked her up and took her outside to the sidewalk. I put her down, held both her hands, and steadied her as she attempted to walk on two feet. I can recall her being happy, excited, and screaming out various words mixed in with "baby talk." I had been holding her hands and letting her go at certain moments to allow her to walk on her own. I'd catch her if she started to tumble. Then all of a sudden, a miracle happened. I let her go, and she started walking perfectly without any help. She no longer needed any help. She made the transition from intellectually knowing that walking is possible to realization (actually walking in real life): hence she walked from that day forward unaided. She continued to walk down the sidewalk as if she knew exactly where she was going. She had almost made it to the other end of the block and kept on walking. As I followed her, I asked, "Hey, where ya going?" She turned around, looked back at me, smiled and kept on. I eventually had to pick her up and take her back to the other end of the block. I was pretty excited myself. I took her inside and showed my mother; mom was thrilled. From that day forward, my niece walked without stumbling. Walking with faith is a similar process. You will have to keep at it. Cultivate it. Finally, the revelation hits you. You are now walking in (the realization) of faith.

Realize Were You Are

You must first realize where you are. There is no way around it. This is where it gets deceptively tricky. Why? Because people lie to themselves. Lying is the same thing as using your words to render yourself powerless. There is power in truth. As the old saying goes, "The truth shall set you free." Likewise, lies will bind and imprison you. Just like the word "faith," that cliché is nothing more than an idle concept in your mind, but the lies are fully active in conscious realization. Before you can have a complete realization of faith, you will have to understand at what stage of development your faith is currently in. Many may think to themselves, ok so I have my ups and downs, therefore, I may still be in "crawling stage" or the "stand up, take a few steps, and stumbling stage." Trust me, if you were really in either of these stages, you'd be producing miracles of biblical proportions. The average human being is not only in the infancy stage, he hasn't even learned to sit up on his own yet. As a matter of fact, he is still struggling with how to hold up his head. Again, you must realize exactly where

The Way of the Warlock

you are because only then can you make an honest start, move forward, and grow.

It's about time to stop using your words to tell yourself lies; wouldn't you say? Why do you lie to yourself? You lie to yourself for various reasons; the following are among the top four.

For reasons of pretense and deceiving others.

You want appear impressive, wise, and strong in front of others.

Delusions of instant gratification.

You are (subconsciously) doubtful that the miracles you were taught to (intellectually) believe can really come true.

You have to gain control of your words; other people, situations, and circumstances are irrelevant. You have to pay attention to the right things. Like my niece in the above scenario, she didn't just sat around watching others walk and complain about not being able to walk; neither did she sit around and lie to herself and others about being able to walk. She understood exactly where she was and continued to cultivate faith. Finally she walked! An excellent start is this:

Maybe you don't know exactly where you are in your faith. Maybe all you know is that you are not getting the results you want. Tell you yourself exactly that particular truth. Simply say, "I do not know what stage of faith I am in; all I know is that I haven't learned to consistently walk yet. I would like to know exactly where I am, so that I can know what my starting point is and start growing."

Do that much and stop right there. You've just made an honest effort; much like my niece when she would pull herself up by using the furniture in the room. Start using your words to tell yourself the truth or see exactly where you are. Whenever you are being pretentious in front of others to appear impressive, catch yourself doing it and tell yourself the truth about it. You can even think to yourself, "Hmmm… I am being pretentious. This is a phony platform. I'd rather be respectfully real."

The Way of the Warlock

You don't have to let others in on it, just keep telling yourself the truth. If you deceive others to take advantage of them, catch yourself and tell yourself the truth, "I am being deceitful. The only reason why I am taking advantage of this person is because I don't honestly think that God will give me exactly what I want at the exact moment I want." What about the miracles you yearn to have. Do you use your words to tell yourself, "What's the use? It's probably too good to be true. It may happen for others, but what are the odds for me?" You really don't have to do this you know. You can disengage.

This is what it all boils down to. You really don't trust God. Face it! Tell yourself the truth! Use your words properly (to your benefit) and all will be well! This is how you gradually rise above intellectual knowing to true realization. If you tell yourself the truth with out fretting or getting upset about the lies and your current condition, then your ascension is assured. Also, there is no need to try and fool yourself or pump yourself up with pretentious positive thinking either. Just remember the following 3 steps:

The Way of the Warlock

1. Catch the lies.
2. Know that you are lying.
3. Don't get upset over the lies.

And that is all there is to it. God will handle the rest. This is where and how the magic really starts to happen. The rising takes care of itself. You are not responsible for the process. If you jump in some water, and you start to sink, the only thing you need to do is position yourself correctly. And you will rise to the surface of the water. Once at the surface, you can breathe again. At that point, simply remain in the correct position. The current of the water will then (eventually) push you toward the safety of the shore. It would be foolish to think that you are responsible for making the water cause you to rise. Those that cannot swim who find themselves in water over their heads, they see the shore in the distance, but don't understand the nature of the water. They panic because they believe themselves to be responsible for making themselves rise. Forcefully trying to think positive equates to the same thing in the mental and spiritual realms. They try to make themselves rise instead of

The Way of the Warlock

allowing themselves to be lifted up and they drown instead of being (effortlessly) taken safely to shore. Again, catch the lies, consciously know that you are lying, and refuse to fret over the lies; this is all that needs to be done. Like my niece who kept steadying herself with furniture, eventually that magical miraculous moment will happen. You will have ascended to the realm of true faith.

A Helpful Tidbit

A wonderful thing to do while you watch yourself lying to yourself is this: watch how you misapply your words to pull the rug out from under your feet. You talk yourself into getting impatient, wondering how long it will take to rise up to the point of realization. Catch yourself in this habitual form of self-sabotage and all will be well. The rising is happening whether it appears to be so or not. Even when under water, you are not able to breathe until you rise to the top, but that doesn't negate the fact that you are rising if you've positioned yourself correctly as mentioned above. Tell yourself the truth, "I am rising (as long as I employ self honesty), and will eventually come to the surface and breathe again because my head will be above the waters of affliction." Self honesty is the way of positioning yourself correctly when immersed in the waters of affliction.

Swimming in the Waters of Affliction

Most people have used their words to create a mindset of impatience. The waters of affliction can be very murky indeed. The murkier the waters, the slower the rise; however, the water is the water and its nature is what it is, and if you position yourself correctly, you will rise. But you can hasten the process if you truly know how to swim. By positioning yourself correctly and paddling, you can speed up the process.

First of all, we need to know what the waters of affliction really are. It is not some troublesome circumstance, bad situation, or rude and evil people that you consistently have to deal with. The "waters of affliction" is a confused, cloudy, paranoid, and fearful mindset. It is characterized by what the author knows to be, "spiritual sleep."

You have used the power of your words to create an alternate (mental) world that clouds over and sometimes completely overshadows or veils the real world that you must deal with. You fear the real world because it doesn't

The Way of the Warlock

match the inner imaginary world that you've created. You must therefore dissolve the inner mental world so that true perception and practical handling of the true outer (real) world can take place. The only way you can ever hope to use your words for yourself instead of against yourself is to obtain true perception of reality. First of all, consider the nature of "spiritual sleep:"

Excerpt from the "Power of Spiritology, Book I

We all know what happens whenever we physically go to sleep. We become unconscious. Shortly after, we start to dream. I have heard people say that they don't have dreams or rarely have dreams, or don't remember their dreams; I've also heard (so-called) experts (on dreams) say that everybody dreams while sleeping whether they know it or not. Let's consider dreaming for a moment. In a nutshell, dreaming is unconscious mental activity giving the appearance of consciousness. You go to sleep, lose consciousness of the outside (physical reality) world, and your (mechanical/subconscious) mind takes you places. Sometimes these places are in the past and sometimes they're in the future. Sometimes reality is distorted or mocked up. It seems real while it's happening, but afterwards we wake up. Sometimes we awaken naturally; sometimes we are jarred out of sleep by some kind of shocking experience during the dream. Once we wake up, we immediately know that we were dreaming because we are now (consciously speaking) back in the real world (physically and mentally). Upon awakening, we can immediately sense the difference between the real world and the dream world; can't we? Well, interestingly enough, people are constantly walking around in a daze; they are partially awake, half awake, some are not even awake at all. An individual experiencing complete "spiritual sleep" can be characterized by a condition known as dementia; most everyone is asleep to some degree. Even while their bodies are up and running in the physical world, men and women all over the place are still unconscious (completely or to some degree). Some people waver back and for between certain degrees of unconsciousness. Think about it. Their minds are still taking them places: to past regrets and pleasantries or future worries and hopeful or dreadful anticipations. And like in real physical sleep, their minds are even mocking up realities. This (mechanical) mental activity seems constant and never ending; correct? Yes, they are up and walking around, conducting business, driving vehicles, fighting and warring with each other, and interacting with each other in numerous ways in the present moment, but their minds are somewhere else (in dreamland); therefore (in a way) they are asleep while awake. This is what is known as spiritual sleep, and if you were to truly wake up or somehow get jarred out of it, you'd immediately know the difference. You'd be a truly decent, happy, and optimum functioning human being. The way to wake up is to see that you are asleep.

How about that? Your words have created an entire world (an inner universe) that only you can see and experience. If there was any reason to doubt the power of words, that reason is now null and void; wouldn't you say?

Here is an interesting fact; just about every other person on the planet has created their very own inner world of make-believe that they retreat into in an effort to hide from (reality) the real world. How can you tell? The answer is nervousness.

People are nervous and apprehensive over everybody and everything.

The reason why you and almost everybody else on the planet are so afraid and nervous is because you have shunned the Creator. You have refused to submit to Him and allow Him to live and govern your life. You and most others (especially those of the Christian faith) have lied and continue to lie about giving your lives over to God. It is an outright blatant satanic lie that you refuse to stop living. This lie in your physic system continues to grow and expand, and as a result, people now suffer from chronic anxiety and even have periodic panic attacks. People (including yourself) may even see other pretenders (perhaps in your church), so in order to not disappoint or upset them, you continue on with the lie and grow stronger in fear. You say that you are a child of God, and if this is so, then you will have to ask yourself, "Why is a spirit of fear and a neurotic mind the only thing I know?" Still think that you are not bewitched (under some sort of sinister sorcery or spell)? If you are religious, then you are spellbound, and an undercover warlock presiding over the church had a lot to do with it. Should you quit your church? Not necessarily, that is a personal decision; however, you should break the spell by being alertly observant. What should you watch for? Watch for the theatrical Holy Ghost possessions. They are in fact demonic trances. After the moment of elation wears off, observe how the possessed individuals go back to their complaining bitterful misery. Then watch them mindlessly mechanically praise God. Watch how they go back and forth. Watch how you (yourself) behave in like fashion. Notice how you lie to yourself.

It even says in the bible that God did not give us a spirit of fear, but of power, love, and a sound mind. [2nd Timothy 1:7]

The Amplified Bible states it like this:

"God did not give us a spirit of timidity (of cowardice, of craven and cringing and fawning fear), but [He has given us a spirit] of power and of love and of calm and well balanced mind and discipline and self-control."

Do you or anyone you know have a well balanced mind: capable of self control? Or do you mechanically spew off in anger (reacting before you can even think about it)? If not, then you are under a spell.

God does not promote fear, trembling, and nervousness. Something else that dwells in you that you've turned your life over to (and compels you to lie) is what makes you cringe and fawn with fear. As far as self control goes, the neurotic mind proves that there is no self control even though you struggle against it by trying to tame outward physical actions and speech.

That's right something else (another force other than God) has gotten a hold on you. But of course you will have some handy excuse to pull out of your hip pocket to justify why you remain in fear as opposed to rising up in faith and living by "grace." You have intellectual knowledge of grace as opposed to realization of grace, but you refuse to admit that, so that you can keep living the lie for the sake of others (and how you appear to them). You'd rather please your pastor, priest, minister, etc… than honor God. Putting others before God is all that the devil ever wanted; this is witchcraft and sorcery in its most diabolical form. And it is overtly

The Way of the Warlock

going on right in the midst of the churches. So the "waters of affliction" (your neurotic mindset) get choppier and more tumultuous. If the truth really be told; you simply do not know what you are doing with your life. You've been trained to lie and pretend every since you were a toddler, so lying is all you know anyway. Some one asks you a question, you give a correct answer and you chalk that up to being truthful or living in the "spirit of truth;" however, nothing could be further from the truth. Now you believe that intellectual knowledge of truth is the same thing as having the true "Spirit of Truth."

Seeing that you are asleep is how you swim in the waters of affliction. Awareness of the murky water is the key. The murky water consists of all the random irrational neurotic action (thoughts) that your mind consistently employs for the sole purpose of obeying the hundreds (perhaps thousands) of faulty, negative, and nonsensical instructions you gave to it by the wrongful usage of your words. Yes, you've made quite a mess of your mind. It's gotten so bad that (often times) you can't pay attention to listen effectively or even think straight. This condition can be arrested and reversed. First thing's first. You must get in touch with the person (your real inner self) that used the power of words to talk your mind into that neurotic state that now creates and shapes your outer world of people, relations, and circumstances. Even physical illnesses you may be struggling with happened because you either used the power of your words against yourself or internalized the devilish words of other people.

Getting in touch with your inner warlock (the observer)

Getting in touch with the observer can be a little tricky at first but once you've done it, you will understand the difference (by way of true realization) between being aware of the real world as opposed to being absorbed in the imaginary world. Every time you make true contact with the inner warlock, you simultaneously calm and clear up the murky waters of affliction. Keep reaching out to the inner warlock because this equates to using the power of your words to tell the inner mental storms to quiet down and be calm.

From a previous book, "The Power of Spiritology, Book I" the author notates the difference between being self-aware and being self-absorbed.

Awareness is a calm seeing of your mental state whereas absorption is being sucked into and hypnotized by your imagination all the while imagining that you are aware. With awareness, negative emotions have no effect on you and can do no harm, but absorption not only carries you away to an inner fantasy land or horror house, but causes you to behave impulsively, mechanically, and destructively. With awareness, you preserve and increase inner strength and physical energy; with absorption, you drain inner strength and physical energy. With practice, you will be able to decipher the difference between the two and thereby hasten your spiritual growth. You must see the difference.

With self awareness you understand that the outside world exists; with self absorption, the only thing that's real for you is the flood of random thoughts, mental scenes, and emotional ups and downs; you are so swept away by this persistent mental activity that you forget you even exist. This is spiritual sleep; jar yourself awake and become aware of the real world as often as possible. This is how you will eventually make initial contact with the warlock within (the magical true self).

The author introduces the observer as the entity you perceive inside your head peeking out at the world from behind the eyeballs. Make it a habit to pause periodically throughout the course of

The Way of the Warlock

your day to pause and be aware of this inner entity. This is a very powerful and edifying thing to do.

Chapter 3
Invocations, Incantations, Rituals, Spells, and Symbols

Hail! Ra! The Mighty Sun God!

Ra was the sun god in ancient Egyptian culture and religion. The Egyptians believed heavily in the power of words. They were very careful and calculated with the words they used and the way they used them, and rightfully so. They fully understood the impact and power that words had over their lives. This is perhaps the number one reason why they were so advanced and ahead of their time. In chapter two, you were told that words could be used to influence the minds, emotions, and behaviors of others, the Egyptians understood this also. But they understood something else beyond the usage of words to influence human affairs. The Egyptians understood something that many claim to understand but take for granted all day every day. They understood that everything you can see and decipher in the realm of physicality had an

The Way of the Warlock

underlying energy and spiritual essence to support it. If this was not so, then it simply couldn't exist. Look in your front yard, perhaps you see a rock. At first glance you may think to yourself, "Oh, it's just a rock: an inanimate dumb object." But is it really? That rock exists by the same power that you yourself exist. I exist because the Creator used the power of His words and called me into existence. He did the very same thing for the rock in your yard. I continue to exist (remain alive) because the Creator is continuously actively thinking about (contemplating) my existence. The same goes for the rock. It remains in existence because the Creator is actively contemplating its existence. God is everywhere present: both inside you and outside you and both inside the rock and outside the rock. This means that just like people, the rock contains spiritual qualities that make it capable of being influenced by the power of words, just like people can be influenced. The Egyptians understood this thoroughly beyond intellectual knowing to the point of realization. The great pyramids are amongst their many accomplishments that even to this day, modern scientists and architects can't figure out how they managed to build these great structures and engineering marvels. The Egyptians understood that spiritual essence (capable of being influenced with words) was in everything. This is why they worshipped so many gods. There were tree gods, river gods, ocean gods, wind gods, etc… These gods were the spiritual essences behind the physical phenomenon.

The Egyptians used the power of words to influence the spiritual essence behind all things physical (not just other human beings) and just like people, every thing else in the environment responded. So were these gods real? The answer is no; they were not real gods. Many ignorant people believe that demons were responsible for assisting the Egyptians, but this too is an erroneous notion. As a matter of fact, it was angels that the Egyptians were invoking. Angels or gods, it may simply be a matter of semantics because the word "angel" may not have been even invented yet; however, the spiritual essence behind everything physical has an angelic presence that holds it in place.

The Way of the Warlock

So along comes a Pharaoh named Akhenaton. He introduces Egypt to monotheism: a religious system of one supreme god overseeing everything. He hailed "Ra" the sun god as the supreme being. Does Ra exist? Of course he does. Is he a real god? Depending on how you look at the word "god," remember we are talking by way of the verbiage of the times back then, but if you consider it in today's language, Ra isn't the supreme being. He is an angelic presence.

"I saw a single angel stationed in the sun's light." (Revelation 19:17 Amplified Bible)

This verse in the bible is perhaps speaking about "Ra," whom the Egyptians considered the supreme being. They thought Ra was the supreme being (perhaps) because they knew what modern science teaches today. Without the sun, nothing would live. All life (and planets) in this solar system would come to an abrupt end. The sun gives (supports) life (the life of you and me and even the life of the rock in your yard). The Egyptians understood that the presence of the sun fully supported and fortified their earthly existence (physical bodies and health) along with everything else. Without the sun, the gods of the rivers, oceans, desserts, and winds, couldn't exist. Ra, the sun god, was superior to all. So what was the sun doing?

If you consider it from a true spiritual perspective, the sun is doing exactly the same thing that God Himself is doing. The angelic presence that dwells in the sun is holding everything (including you and me and all the planets) together in the entire solar system by way of its gravitational pull. It is constantly (unselfishly) giving us its light and healing energies. It never stops to ask for anything else in return. It just keeps on giving to all (the just and the unjust). Its rays not only fortify our skin with the vitamin "D" that it requires, but it even seeps down to the core of our bones which also requires vitamin "D." Plants, fruits, and herbs get their energy, vitamins, and other life giving and healing properties from the sun by way of a process science calls "photosynthesis." They absorb the sun's light and transmute it into the nourishment we build our physical bodies with by ingesting them. In more ways than you know, the sun is constantly radiating its light unconditionally for all: giving us the gift of (earthly) life. Akhenaton (perhaps) realized this, and this could be why he proclaimed Ra (the angel that operates the sun) the supreme being; however, the sun is only an angel. God Himself called it forth when He decreed, "Let there be light." How did He do it? With His words.

An angel is the "word of God" in action. Angels are formed directly by the words of the Creator. They are God's words made manifest in physical or energetic forms and bodies. Now they are already in place (on standby) to act (do the will of God) on behalf of the words of the warlock. God has set everything in place; your job is to use your words correctly.

Yet and still, we are not attempting to promote worshipping the sun or angels; however, the author wishes to convey that religion at that time was headed in a certain direction. At this point, religion was still growing into maturity. At this point (like in the example of my niece) it

The Way of the Warlock

was picking itself up, using various pieces of furniture (like the rivers, oceans, winds, and even the sun) to steady itself as it prepared to finally walk. The Egyptians were able to connect with angels. This is why they were so ahead of their time; however, be that as it may, (maybe) religion was in its adolescent stage. They hadn't quite connected with the true "Supreme Being," but they were close.

It can be compared to living in a household with siblings. When I was still in elementary school, I couldn't understand or do certain things like homework assignments; my brother, being four years older than I, understood what I was dealing with perfectly, so he was able to help me out, not only with school work, but with other things that I needed help with. However, his ability to assist me was limited. When it came to everything he did for me, there were things that he couldn't do. At that time, he wasn't putting food on the table or clothes on my back. My father was. I could go to my father for not only the things my brother did for me, but practically every need I could conceive of, I could go to him (directly to

The Way of the Warlock

the source). In a way, the Egyptians were getting help from (big brothers) in the spiritual realm. But the way of the warlock is to go directly to the source. Going to the source; this is where the power of words really come into play. Words were used by the Egyptians and are used today by every type of religious faction in an effort to petition the Source of all things.

Many think that magic is of the devil and believed that the Egyptians worshipped and invoked demons, but the truth is that they renounced evil and used words to keep demons at bay and rebuke them. They used magic to ward off demons.

Incantations, invocations, and certain rituals that include spells and usage of symbols all involved words that supposedly had power instilled within to influence the Creator much in the same way we use them to influence other people. A true warlock is no different when it comes to using words. Although many people take words and the way they use them for granted, the warlock knows the true value of words, and like the Egyptians, he treasures them and uses them wisely.

So let's get to the crux of this particular chapter: Incantations, invocations, and rituals. We will start off with the definitions of each.

Incantation defined: use of supposedly magic words: the ritual chanting or use of supposedly magic words.

Invocation defined: calling upon higher power: a calling upon a greater power such as God or a spirit for help: prayer: a short prayer forming part of a religious service.

Invocation even has an opposite counterpart: supposedly summoning demons: a casting of a spell in an attempt to make an evil spirit appear, or the spell itself (but this particular meaning will not have any merit for the theme of this manuscript).

Ritual defined: has multiple meanings that points the way to a common basic definition, that is "repetitious patterns of behavior," so for the context of this book we will use the one that serves its

The Way of the Warlock

purpose; therefore a ritual is "established formal behavior: an established and prescribed pattern of observance, as in a religion"

Spell defined: words with supposed magical power: a word or series of words believed to have magical power, spoken to invoke the magic: influence of magic words: the influence that a spell has over somebody or something: fascination: a compelling fascination or attraction (this last meaning will be touched upon later).

Symbol defined: something that represents something else: something that stands for or represents something else, especially an object representing an abstraction: in Egyptian culture; symbols were just as important as words. If the real thing wasn't around a symbol was used and it was taken as a worthy substitute for the real thing that it represented.

Words themselves are even symbols. If I say the word "dog" to you, the word itself is not a real dog. It is symbolic of a dog, but the verbal symbol has power because it prompts the image of a dog (perhaps your very own) to populate your mind's creative space. I can even use more symbols (in the form of words) to construct a more detailed image in an effort to give you a more specific picture because I wish influence you (your thoughts) to match my very own. For instance I can say, "The dog is a big brown and black German Shephard." Now you have a more detailed image and you are thinking just what I want you to and the exact way I want you to.

If you consider a sermon in a church, the very same thing is happening. A minister is using symbols (words) to influence your imagination; you therefore construct imaginary pictures of events and people (inside your head) based upon the way he uses his words. Although, you were not there and couldn't possibly know what was really done and said, you are being influenced to think exactly what and the way he or she wants you to. In truth, this is the way the stereotypical warlock grains

The Way of the Warlock

power over the masses. He carefully uses words that are infused with the energy of emotion, and this energy coupled with the symbols (words) gets translated into your very own mindspace. You now believe that his thoughts are your very own. This is how many people are blindly influenced and therefore controlled by others. It's not just happening within the church as you will later see.

Sometimes if a worthy symbol wasn't handy, the Egyptians would use a papyrus (a type of thick paper produced from a papyrus plant) with words written on them to substitute. Words were pretty much the crux of the matter when it came to Egyptian magic.

The following is a series of incantations, invocations, spells, rituals, with recommended symbols. You are welcome try them; the author makes no guarantees for you; however, he has performed and experimented with success by using them.

The Way of the Warlock

If you are a practicing (traditional organized) Christian; don't be too hasty to judgment. After all, Christianity blatantly and overtly does it all, and all the while condemns others from doing the same. Even if you are not catholic, your church may ritualistically recite the Lord's Prayer or even some of the psalms of King David. Do you realize that both of these are types of invocations and incantations (attempts to use words to directly influence God)? You may even use words to sing hymns as part of your rituals. But of course, what church doesn't use symbols like crucifixes or imaginary pictures of Jesus? Does your church (if you attend) have images of dead saints or the Virgin Mary hanging or painted on the wall or engrained in stained glass windows? If so, then nothing that you are about to read next is any different from anything you already practice. These are symbols, and they are there on the walls and windows to serve as substitutes for the real thing. Keep an open mind, especially if you suffer from a neurotic mind.

The Way of the Warlock

Note: each incantation should be repeated 3 times unless otherwise instructed. But first write down the incantation on a piece of paper in your very own hand writing (this helps to reinforce the power of the words by helping to engrain them into your mind). Next, silently read over the incantation. Afterwards, try to visualize as best as possible what it is you'd like the incantation to do for you. Next recite 3 times aloud as instructed. Your verbalized words are being sent out and actually cause vibrations in the spiritual atmosphere where God will hear and instruct the angels exactly how to take heed of them. Then visualize your desire as accomplished: unless otherwise instructed.

Incantations

If you consider a sermon in a church, the very same thing is happening. A minister is using symbols (words) to influence your imagination; you therefore construct imaginary pictures of events and people (inside your head) based upon the way he uses his words. Although, you were not there and couldn't possibly know what was really done and said, you are being influenced to think exactly what and the way he or she wants you to. In truth, this is the way the stereotypical warlock grains power over the masses. He carefully uses words that are infused with the energy of emotion, and this energy coupled with the symbols (words) gets translated into your very own mindspace. You now believe that his thoughts are your very own. This is how many people are blindly influenced and therefore controlled by others. It's not just happening within the church as you will later see.

The Way of the Warlock

Sometimes if a worthy symbol wasn't handy, the Egyptians would use a papyrus (a type of thick paper produced from a papyrus plant) with words written on them to substitute. Words were pretty much the crux of the matter when it came to Egyptian magic.

Incantation for Infusing Power into your Words and Utterances

First thing's first. Before you can really start to use incantations your words must contain power to accomplish whatever the individual incantation is meant to bring to pass. Therefore, the following incantation is for the purpose of doing just that and getting you on the road to manifestation.

My words are irresistible
My voice cannot be denied
Whatever I say must come to pass
With sustained intention applied

My words literally shake the heavens
The earth is made to rumble
The sound of my voice is a force like thunder
The vibrations make mountains crumble

The Lord hears my words always
For they are loud and clear
He grants my each and every request
By way of angels far and near

The Way of the Warlock

Incantation for Self Crucifixion and Ascension

This incantation is designed to release the devil from the psyche and heal the troubled mind. Right now, you are at one with the devil if your mind is troubled. The devil is masquerading as your very spirit to where you can't tell the difference between the "I" that is your real spirit and the "I" that has concealed your spirit and is impersonating it, so self crucifixion is in order. You are compelling the devil to put himself up to be executed and ousted from within your vessel so that your true spirit can be reborn.

Father Christ crucify me
So the devil may not persecute me

Lord Almighty crucify me
Let not satan execute me
Father Christ purify me
That I may incessantly commune with thee

Lord my God, before you I bow
Remove the devil from this vessel now!

Thank you father for hearing my voice

The Way of the Warlock

The devil has gone; he had no choice
Thank you Father for crucifying me
I am reborn and ascending to thee!

Do this ritual as often as you feel
necessary; afterwards, (with this
particular one) be sure to not image how
the spiritual rebirth will take place or
even what it will feel like; otherwise you
will resurrect the devil back into your
spiritual home. Keep this in mind for any
other incantation you may wish to try;
just do your best to employ the emotions
of expectancy. This goes for all of the
incantations that are about inner
transformation. As far as the ones that
are for transforming worldly
circumstances, then visualization is
totally warranted.

The Way of the Warlock

Incantation for total Mind/Body Clearing and Healing

Clear me God
Clear me up

Heal this body
Cleanse this mind

Your Holy Ghost
Let my spirit find

Clear me God
Clear me up

Heal this body
Cleanse this mind

Your Holy Ghost
Let my spirit find

Thank you Lord for hearing me
I praise you Father for clearing me!

Incantation for Mental Clarity

Let the Lord grant me true perception
Let my spirit plainly see

Give to me perfect reception
Allow me true reality

Unclutter my mind
Remove all falsity

Restore my consciousness
Back to pure reality

Thank You Father Christ
for restoring my spiritual sight

Thank you Lord God
For giving me Your Light

I praise you Father Christ
For giving me spiritual sight

Thank You Lord God
For the precious gift of Your Light

Incantation for Casting out the Devil

The devil can manifest in a multitude of ways and forms. He can present himself as a troubled mindset or a troublesome person. He can manifest as an adverse circumstance, disease, even a neighbor's ornery pet or unruly child. Visualize what your life would be like without the vexation and then perform the incantation.

This particular incantation is to be done out loud; the final verse is to be repeated 7 times. Satan's presence (in the mind) can prove to be a formidable stronghold for many people, much like the "Walls of Jericho." Therefore, it is advised to say the incantation and give the final (mighty shout) 7 times over.

Satan be gone!
Devils get away from me
I have nothing to do with thee!

Satan be gone!
From my presence you must flee!
In the name of Christ I command thee!

Satan, with a mighty shout!
In the name of the Lord, I cast you out!

The Way of the Warlock

Satan, with a mighty shout!
In the name of the Lord, I cast you out!

Satan, with a mighty shout!
In the name of the Lord, I cast you out!

Satan, with a mighty shout!
In the name of the Lord, I cast you out!

Satan, with a mighty shout!
In the name of the Lord, I cast you out!

Satan, with a mighty shout!
In the name of the Lord, I cast you out!

Satan, with a mighty shout!
In the name of the Lord, I cast you out!

The Way of the Warlock

Incantation for Rejuvenation
For feelings of chronic fatigue and
lethargy

In the name of Christ the Light I decree
Father in heaven please refresh me

Restore my body
calm my mind

Divine strength and energy
Let this vessel find

Lift me up, in freedom and grace
Instill my consciousness into your
heavenly place

In the name of Christ the Light I decree
Let your ministering angels comfort me

In the name of Christ the Light I decree
Thank you Father for reviving me

Incantation for World and Air Bending
Manifesting Miracles

This particular incantation (the author believes) is very similar to the types that the Egyptians used when building the great pyramids, constructing the magnificent obelisks, and forming the mighty majestic sphinx. Moses, who was raised in Egypt, understood "world bending" completely when he told the Israelites, "Stand still, and behold the salvation of the Lord!" The Red Sea parted, making a dry path of land for the Israelites to cross over. Of course it goes without saying that "air bending" at its finest was demonstrated when Christ Himself uttered the infamous, "Peace, be still!" and calmed the storm. Last but not least, probably the most notable of all honorable mentions (if it does not one up the previous demonstrations) is that of Joshua when he shouted out,

"Sun, be silent and stand still at Gibeon, and you, moon, in the valley of Ajalon!"

And the sun stood still and the moon stayed. The sun stood still in the midst of the heavens and did not hasten to go down for a whole day. (Book of Joshua 10:12 Amplified Bible)

This may be the greatest example of world bending ever conceived. All this being said, world and air bending have typically been accomplished by only those "masters" that were well advanced on the path of "spiritual development;" however, the words below contain immense potential and power for anyone wishing to develop to the point of world and air bending.

The world is like putty in my hands
Even the wind and rain obey my commands

In the name of the supreme God anything is possible

My words penetrate like sharp rods that are unstoppable

The world molds itself to my commands and decrees

Physicality submits and falls to its knees

The world is only clay, to be shaped with my hands

In the name of the supreme God, it obeys my commands!

The Way of the Warlock

Incantation for Mind over Matter

Mind over matter is like a sibling to air and world bending. In truth, mind and matter are tightly interwoven with one another. As a matter of fact, mind is infused into all matter. It is something akin to a spiritual glue that holds matter into place (matter is mind condensed into solid form). If properly understood, we can realize that our very own individual minds are one with (woven into) the Grand Universal Mind of the Creator Whose infinitely colossal Mind permeates everything. By true realization that our mind is part of the Mind that holds it all together, we ourselves can manipulate, change, and control matter by a process of conscious contemplation and thinking. After all, a simple act of getting up and walking across the room is a minute example of mind over matter: your body being the matter and your conscious willful contemplation of walking being the controlling thought mechanism. The only thing required to move matter with our will that is independent of our physical bodies is a greater realization of these spiritual facts and truths.

The Way of the Warlock

I attribute the power to where it belongs
My thoughts grow ever so strong

Physicality being temporal cannot resist
My most dominant desires that tend to
persist

No matter how solidly grounded
Or strong it appears to be

I command any mountain before me
Be uprooted and cast into the sea

In the name of Christ the Light
You cannot resist me!

The Way of the Warlock

Incantation for seeing through Fear

Fear is what it all boils down to. It is the sole reason for the invention of religion. Man fears he cannot control his life so he uses religion to foster (illusory) control of life by controlling other people. He does not know God so he attempts to be a god. If man was not afraid of life (living and experiencing it fully or losing it) or uncertain about the world he lives in there'd be no need for religion or any other system of discovering and relating to God. It is the truly fearless mind that has discovered and united with God. The irony is that religion has completely backfired on mankind; like added gasoline to flames, religion has (collectively) caused the fires of fear to blaze completely out of control. Mankind has no clue whatsoever as to how to extinguish it. The following incantation is for the purpose of dousing your very own personal mental wildfire that is fear:

Since God is not the author of fear,
It cannot truly be real

No illusion can therefore vex my mind
Now let my perception heal

In the name of Christ the Light,
I hereby cast out fear

By the power of God vested in me,
I decree my mind is clear!

Incantation for Perfect Health and Vigor

As superficial as it sounds, many people see life as being pointless if you have to endure it with a body that suffers. Most have had one ailment or another. Certain illnesses like allergies are considered minute and can be endured without much perceived inconvenience; however, there have been filthy rich folks (confined to sickbeds) that would've given their very last dollar to know the joys of a healthy body. Ultimately, money can't buy health, but the right words of power can restore or perpetuate good health, hence the very next incantation:

This body is a temple of God
It is perfect and can't be sick
It is a living (animated) house of God
Divinely constructed with spiritual bricks

A true house of God cannot fall
Its foundation is solidly secure
This temple of God is packed with
power
Any attack upon it cannot endure

In the name of Christ the Light,
I declare this body healthy and strong
Let the power of God keep it
So nothing could ever go wrong

Incantation for Money and Abundant Financial Blessings

When it comes to money and religious faith, a paradox seems to be in order. We are taught not to covet money but to seek after God instead. The confusion sets in because the church itself is always hungrily seeking after money. Many churches so lustfully chases after dollars that they don't even seem to care or realize that they are driving their congregations to the poorhouse. This is not the way God meant it to be. You were meant to have more than enough money to live a comfortable lifestyle: to be able to do what you want whenever you want and likewise go wherever you want. The warlock completely understands that money is a tool to be used, not an idol to be worship. He therefore has abundance and simultaneously keeps his lot (spiritually speaking) in its proper perspective. Filled with the Spirit of God Himself, the warlock can never succumb to devilish mindsets like greed. He gives generously and likewise receives.

Money is a necessity
It's foolish to deny its need
In the name of the Lord it flows to me
abundantly
My requirements it exceeds

In the name of Christ the Light
I have enough money for a comfortable
life
In the name of God the Father
There is no financial struggling or strife

Thank you Father in heaven
Your spirit of abundance I muse
I thank you in the name of Christ
For giving me more money than I can
use

Incantation for finding a Helpmate

"And God said that it is not good that man be alone;" we all know the story of Adam and Eve written in the book of Genesis. We all have that innate desire for perfect companionship. It was not meant for neither man nor woman to travel this earthly journey alone. The next incantation is designed to do just what the doctor ordered; of course if you are a woman reading this, you will substitute the word "woman" and install the word "man."

Ideal woman I decree
Perfect woman made for me
Come to me my perfect mate
Come to me now don't hesitate
I need you now, I need no longer wait
In the name of the Lord, appear my
helpmate

Ideal woman I decree
Perfect woman made for me
It is the will of God for you and me
By the power of Christ so let it be!

We have pretty much covered it all as
far as life is concerned with the
preceding incantations and invocations.
Any concern or worry that you have
should fall under at least one of them.
So we will now move on to…

Spells

Typically when a spell is thought of, the verbiage is what usually throws people (especially the religious) for a loop: the association being with witches and black magic. It conjures up fear and trepidation with paranoid expectations of satan or one of his devils being released to come into and destroy your life. In conjunction with the literal meaning, it can be easily seen that priests make usage of spells to cast out devils. They call it "exorcism." But they use specialized words and phrases; they even use symbolic props like crucifixes and holy water, which by the way was blessed by using a spell. They supposedly install "spiritual" power into the water. In a way, even "baptism" is something like a spell being cast, but it's not looked at in that light. Again, the church in all of its hypocritical glory forbids its congregations from a practice that its leaders completely indulge in.

The author has not done so much by way of spells; meaning that he hasn't employed them as much as he has used incantations and invocations. However, the few times that he has used them,

The Way of the Warlock

they proved to be successful. So we will provide you with a few spells, but keep in mind that you can create your very own. The previous dialogue on "spells" (holy water) will bring us to our very first one.

How to make and use Holy Water

The church, especially Catholicism believes that they have the market corned on this particular practice, but nothing could be further from the truth. You can make your very own "holy water" and use it to be a source of blessing for you and your family. Get a twelve ounce bottle or jar. Make sure that it is made of glass and has a lid or cap to keep it secure. The ideal lid should be made of cork. However, it's not mandatory. Fill the container up with twelve ounces of distilled water. Wash your hands thoroughly and get a bottle of extra virgin olive oil. Dab a little bit of the oil on your index finger. Just a touch; a full drop would be too much. Next, dab the inside of the cork or cap of the bottle with your finger, so that a small smear of the oil is on it. This is symbolic of anointing the physical vessel. The water inside is symbolic of the now sanctified (uncontaminated) spiritual essence contained in the physical vessel. Secure the cap on the bottle. Next, recite the following incantation 3 times:

In the name of the Lord, I bless this
water
I declare it liquid light
In the name of the Father, this water is
now holy
By the power of His might

After you do this, place the water bottle
on a balcony or in a window; where it
can be soaked with the rays of the sun.
It is best to place the water so that it
faces the sunrise (this infuses it with
divine power and energy). At about
noon, the water can be taken from its
spot in the sun; if it can't be taken down
by noon because of inconveniences like
having to be at work, it doesn't hurt it to
stay there all day until you get home; it
can be placed in the refrigerator. It can
be used to anoint yourself or others. It
can even be ingested for blessing you
with physical health.

Spell for Protection (for you or a loved one)

Cinnamon acts as a shield to ward off evil spirits; bad intentions and entrapments: get two cinnamon sticks. One should be maybe three inches long and the other two inches long. Next form a crucifix with them. The shorter stick should be the one that "crosses the 'T.'" You can use a small rubber band or even a "twistee tie" used to seal loaves of bread or one that is used to close up trash bags will suffice. Also, before you secure it with the band or twistee, you may want to bore a groove into both sticks that is wide as each stick is thick. Fasten the cross together by way of the grooves. This helps to prevent a wobbly cross. If you don't have a rubber band or twistee, then a small dab of glue will suffice.

After you've made your cross, recite over it the following words 3 times:

The Way of the Warlock

In this world that is uncertain and
stressed
The Lord watches over me, I am
incessantly blessed
This world I fear not, and neither do I
fight
For I am secure and protected by God
and the power of His might

You can display it somewhere handy
that you will get a glimpse of it everyday
like on top of a shelf or coffee table or
dresser drawer. If you are more of a
private person, then perhaps you can
put it inside the medicine cabinet in a
bathroom or sock drawer. It would be a
good décor piece also to display on the
rear view mirror of your car or in the
glove compartment to ward off traffic
accidents and being pulled over by the
police. Or you can simply give it to
someone that you care about; you don't
have to necessarily tell them what it's
for. If the cross is for another person,
use the person's name in the
incantation; also don't forget to write it
down in your own hand writing first.
Envision yourself, your home, car, or
even the other person surrounded by a
globe of protective white light.

The Way of the Warlock

Please be mindful of your very own behavioral tendencies. For instance, if you are driving on the highway and you are intentionally violating traffic laws, if you are participating in illegal activity in your home, you will began to deplete from your surroundings the protective energy. Angels will not be dispatched to go to the aid of someone indulging in willful demonic intent. Also, remember that the cross itself is a symbol. What it does is to serve as a reminder that you are divinely protected. The reason why you are encouraged to put it somewhere that you will see it daily is because human nature tends to forget to think about or count blessings; therefore, you will be reminded of God's protection on a constant basis. The daily reminder helps to not only reinforce the protection but it gets more and more powerful as you more and more contemplate it.

The Way of the Warlock

Spell for Blessings

The only thing truly needed is a bottle of extra virgin olive oil. The oil is for anointing or you can even use the "holy water" from the previous spell, if you've made any. You can do this for yourself or another person. If you are blessing someone else and they are not around, you can use a picture.

Olive oil is already known for its health promoting qualities. Recite the incantation 3 times:

May the Lord bless this oil
By the power of His might
Whosoever it anoints
Shall be filled with goodness and light

Take a dab of the oil and trace a crucifix on your forehead and over your heart. If you are blessing someone else and they are not around. Get a picture of the person and anoint a dab of the oil on the forehead of the person in the picture.

Spell for Good Health

Tea tree oil is a good oil for this particular spell; however, even olive oil or almond oil are worthy substitutes, if no tea tree oil is available. You will need maybe half a pinch of garlic powder too. Both garlic and tea tree oil are known for their healing properties. Garlic has also been said to have the power to ward off evil spirits. It was used centuries ago, to keep away blood sucking vampires. This tradition more than likely came about because it has been known to be an effective mosquito repellant. The author has personal experience with garlic as a source of personal blessing. He once caught a severe cold. He decided to have a bowl of chicken soup. He decided to spice it up with lemon pepper, but he didn't have any in the cupboard. All he could find was garlic powder, so he sprinkled some generous shakes into the soup. The cold (along with the accompanying congestion) cleared up in a matter a few hours. He went to work the next morning as good as new.

Take a half pinch of the garlic powder and mix it with a cap full of the tea tree oil. Depending on how big the cap is, you really don't need much; about 4 drops will suffice. After you've created the mixture, recite the incantation 3 times.

Let blessed robust health be mine
Let healing power flow to me from the Divine

In the name of Christ I declare I am free
From any infirmity that seeks to vex me
Thank you Father for letting it be

Take the mixture and trace a crucifix over your heart and forehead. If you have an ailment already, draw a third crucifix over the ailing part of the body. Like in the previous spell, you can use a picture of someone if doing it for another. If doing it on yourself, immediately go wash the potion off (as Christ instructed the blind man to go wash the mud from his eyes thereby regaining his sight).

Why are incantations, invocations, rituals, and spells necessary?

Incantations, invocations, rituals, and spells are necessary because we are spiritual creatures enclosed in physical vessels. We therefore need a method of tangibility to connect to the Spirit of God beyond the surface of our skin. Look at it like this. As of now, you don't realize it but, you are indirectly connecting to the people around you. You are not making direct connections. You may hug a loved one in an effort to show them love and support. However, the gist of the matter is that your hug is symbolic of the attempt of your spiritual essence's attempt to connect with theirs. When you hug a loved one, you feel the vibrations and pulsations of their inner energy connecting with yours. You share each others energy and invigorate one another. During the hug, the physical flesh serves as a bridge to connect your spirits. Likewise, you can call someone over the telephone (who may be a thousand miles away) and use words to serve the same purpose of connecting with and invigorating each other's spirits. In this case, the tangible (audible) words install the connection.

The Way of the Warlock

Bridging the gap between the spiritual and the physical is the purpose of incantations, invocations, rituals, and spells.

With regard to incantations and invocations: don't worry whether or not they will work or if they are working… you've got nothing to lose and everything to gain. The goal is to not dump more poison (in the guise of worry and doubt) into the solution. These are mostly for beginners, as an advanced warlock you will simply be able to call forth that which you desire and bypass the "middle man" of ceremonies and incantations.

A Basic Love Spell for Men

(Women can do it too; just substitute a male figure in place of the female figure that is in the spell's demonstration). Let's say you encounter a woman that you are interested in. **If you are seeking to use her for gratification, or if she is in a committed relationship, then this spell is not recommended**. It could very well backfire on you in a negative way. If you are genuine with your intentions, but she doesn't seem to notice or be attracted to you, then take heed to the following:

In your mind's eye, visualize yourself with the woman on a date in a familiar environment: like on the sofa in your living room watching a movie; next hear her distinctively say, "Thank you for allowing me to come over." You can hear yourself respond with a "you're welcome" or something of the sort. It's important for her to verbalize her words in the exact manner as indicated because this indicates that she is pursuing you. You are not chasing her. Otherwise you could be compelled to do something dumb or make a fool of yourself and turn her off. Visualize this scene in the morning as soon as you wake up before you even get out of bed. Do this on a Monday, Wednesday, and Friday. Try not to think about whether it is working or not on the days and times in between. Afterwards, on the following week, visualize her waking up next to you in bed, smiling, and saying good morning to each other. Then give each other a kiss (peck on the lips) before you get up to start your day. Do this also on a Monday, Wednesday, and Friday. Make the scenes and vivid as possible. In the meantime in the real world, try to be around her as much as possible, say "Hello" or make small talk if the opportunity presents itself. If she is very beautiful, do not venture into the realm of giving complements. She is probably used to it and it may cause a barrier to the spell in the form of her taking you as a typical man. Be nonchalant but polite. Don't go out of your way, but if the opportunity is there, open doors for her or perform other polite but manly gestures. You are to perform these actions from here on out combined with the alternating weeks of the visualizations. To your pleasant surprise, she should eventually suggest that you do something together. Don't

be overzealous. Just let things flow in a
natural way. And keep up with both the
actions and the visualizations, and the
love of your life will eventually be
yours. Also, keep another factor in mind.
This person may not be the one for you;
if she is, then she will come to you;
however, if she isn't meant for you, then
keep up with the spell anyway. She is a
symbol that represents the ideal woman
for you; keep it up and the perfect girl
(meant for you) will appear whenever
you least expect it.

The Way of the Warlock

Curses

The bible teaches that curses are ill advised. It also teaches that an undeserved curse will boomerang back to the one who initiated it. Curses are dangerous because they require the negative energies of anger or hostile vindictiveness that have sources rooted in the presence of demons. If someone is vexing you or your life in a really bad way then you can supplement the blessing of your self with a "cast away ritual."

The following is a "cast away" ritual from a previous book by the author entitled, "The Power of Alchemy, The Higher Science of God." If you are compelled to use it, please follow the instructions very carefully, otherwise you could be a victim of some very negative karma. The cast away spell is entitled,

"Troublesome People"

Troublesome people could very well be the number one obstacle to anyone's progress. It's a known fact that people prey off of each other: mentally, physically, and emotionally. They are not satisfied unless they are manipulating, controlling, using, or even abusing others. First and foremost, you must be sure that you don't fall into any of the categories above. First check your very own thinking, behavior patterns, and habits to ensure that you are not a predator (physically, mentally, and emotionally) preying on others. Next you must then release yourself from others that may be preying upon you: you must cease to be a victim. Here is how. This particular exercise is for a person that you really don't need in your life. Let's say you have a troublesome person in your life that is hindering your progress or making you miserable, what you should do is vividly see that person in your imagination. Make the image as vivid, colorful, and lifelike as possible. Imagine that the person is facing you and looking you in the eye. Now imagine that person smiling at you (sincerely) then hear in your mind's ear that person saying "Goodbye, I am leaving you forever now." After this, imagine that the person turns around and starts walking away. As the person walks away, gradually let the scene fade from color to black and white. By the time the individual is about 20 feet away, the scene should be completely black and white. Watch as the person disappears over the horizon. Now, let the scene go completely black. After this happens, say silently or verbally, "Good bye forever, and may the grace and peace of God be with you." The blessing is very crucial and should not be forgotten otherwise this exercise (even though it will still work) could very well comeback to haunt you in a negative way. If you don't bless the other person then you fall into the realm of witchcraft or black magic, [you wouldn't want the person to go away by means of a tragic accident of some sort] so be mindful to bless. Also, self honesty is very important when you are checking yourself. For instance if someone is vexing you at work, and you tend to go home and take it out on others, then you'd be better off not doing this ritual unless you first ask God for forgiveness, next go to the other person, apologize, and ask for

The Way of the Warlock

forgiveness, if they forgive you (verbally) then you can proceed with the ritual and rid yourself of the troublesome person; however, if they don't forgive, but choose to stubbornly hold a grudge, and your apology and forgiveness request were sincere, then the negative energy is theirs to keep; you have washed your hands clean of the matter (dispensed with the bad energy), hence you can proceed with the ritual.

Usage of Spells in Everyday Life

When it comes to spells and their usage, it is very crucial that you remain alert and aware of yourself and your surroundings. You could be under a spell at this very moment and not even realize it. People are casting spells upon each other day in and day out without truly understanding what they are doing. Here is a real life example of a common everyday spell being cast:

One day I was at a car rental establishment picking up a car that I had rented online. As I listened to the sales rep review the terms of the rental agreement, he started talking about car insurance. I really didn't want to get the insurance because I wasn't going to be putting a lot of miles on the car; however, he started talking about the possibilities of having an accident and not being covered should one occur. Through repeatedly talking about having an accident, the possibility of having one finally crossed my mind, and I bought the insurance (the "basic" package) and it turned out to cost more than the car rental itself. A "rip off?" No doubt, however, a spell was cast and I was influenced into doing exactly what he wanted me to do. Later that same night, I was watching the evening news. The news caster kept on with repetitious reports of the same crimes, accidents, and negative events. I watched as some family members looked on with deep looks of concern and remarked with common clichés like, "What's this world coming to? People are going crazy, etc…" The news casters were getting inside their heads: casting spells. I thought to myself, "In actuality, they really are spell casters as opposed to news casters." This is no different from what stereotypical witches do. I've often seen ministers up in pulpits do the same thing to extract money from congregations. Again, be aware of your surroundings and try to see if you can spot any type of spells being cast.

The Way of the Warlock

How Do Spells Work

As you can see from reading the previous section, spells work by a phenomenon known as "hypnosis." It is by way of the "power of suggestion." The power of suggestion works simply because an individual is incapable of properly and consistently guarding his mind. The same goes with the usage of "imagery" whenever you want another to do something on your behalf. Most people lack the ability to exercise complete control of their own minds and this is why they are vulnerable to spells. If you recall the previous segments on "spiritual sleep" and "nervousness" then you'll understand completely why people don't have self-mind control. Spiritual sleep, neurosis, and nervousness all go hand in hand and are all indications of a mind that is out of control. And an out of control mind is a vulnerable and susceptible mind. If you have a susceptible mind, then you tend to believe in what you are being told or whatever is happening to you. It is the belief that sets the power of manifestation in motion and causes the spell to come true.

In the rental car scenario, it is a safe bet that God doesn't condone automobile accidents; I could've trusted Him to keep me safe and gone about my business; however, I became susceptible to the agent's suggestions of an accident. I accepted it as a possibility and "Whammo!" A spell was cast; I bought the coverage.

A spell basically uses the power of your very own faith (sometimes coupled with the "spell caster's" faith) to manifest whatever the spell calls for. If someone casts a spell over you or on your behalf, what is happening is this: you have given someone else authority over your very own God given power to either create or hinder your life. You have spiritually shut yourself down and made the other person (witch, warlock, or even priest or minister) into a false God. Religious folks tend to do this when they ask others to pray for them. They know that their faith is weak, so they attribute false power, virtue, and strength to others. If you need to ask someone to pray on your behalf, why not ask God Himself to pray for you? When looked at in this light, it should motivate you to reclaim your power.

The Way of the Warlock

Thought Transference

Another type of spell is that of "thought transference;" another way of saying it is mental telepathy. It is similar to the technique used in the "Love Spell for Men" segment. When talking to someone, think of something that you'd like them to do or know. Look him in the eye, for a period of time without blinking and think the thought you want to infuse into his head. If you want him to do something (like give you money) then while conversing with him on an unrelated matter, look him in the eye and without blinking mentally say, "_____ needs 'x' amount of dollars. Give it to him." Fill in the blank with your name. If you have the same name as other people he may know, then use your first and last name (middle name too if need be). Make the thought as loud and clear in your head as possible, and continue on with the conversation. The thought should be planted in his head. He will now believe that it was his very own thought. He should proceed to act it out and give you money.

Spell of Protection against Mental Hacking

Ok it was said that many people are walking around with their minds fully exposed. They are vulnerable to be attacked. It's called "mind hacking." You do not have to succumb to it; you can prevent yourself from being infiltrated. Heed the following spell.

Imagine your brain inside of your head being filled with a bright yellow light. Make it so bright that the glow's beams come shining forth from out of your ears, nose, and eyes. Next recite the following incantation 3 times.

My mind is a sacred ground
Filled with God's protective light
My mind is clear and sound
Its safety is my divine right
My mind is my personal space.
No one can invade it or infiltrate.
My mind is a private place.
No foreign thoughts can penetrate.
In the name of the Heavenly Father
Protect my sacred ground
By the power of His might
Let my mind be safe and sound

The Way of the Warlock

Chapter 4: How to Make and Use a Magic Wand

This book would be somewhat remiss if we didn't touch up on a bit of the traditional type of magic, so we will do just that and show you how to make a magic wand.

We've all seen the Disney cartoons and other such television programs with good witches, fairy god mothers and such. They wielded magic wands that could instantly make wishes come true. Interestingly enough, through out history, magic wands have been used to work magic or create miracles with reports of astonishing success. The Pharaohs of Egypt and their priests had staffs that supposedly possessed magic powers. As a matter of fact, the entire religious belief systems of ancient Egypt revolved around magic. As mentioned earlier, Moses, who was raised in Egypt, was said to have wielded a "Sapphire Staff." I'm not certain how this rumor came about; however, I do recall in the scripture that he did have a Sheppard's staff. Perhaps it had undergone some sort of transformation when he

The Way of the Warlock

encountered the angel of the Lord within the "burning bush." If this rumor is true, then even without the magic power, the staff itself would've made for a very magnificent spectacle: sapphire being a precious stone of brilliant blue color. This staff would've been most impressive. The sapphire staff was mentioned for a practical purpose because the wand you are about to be shown how to make should possess a quality of sapphire just like Moses' staff. Therefore, you will need...

A small stud sized sapphire stone (you can use a substitute imitation blue stone for as you recall a symbol will work just as the real thing)

A wood rod about 16 to 20 inches long and 2 to 3 inches in circumference: it should taper off to a rounded off point on one end; the wood should preferably come from an olive or almond branch; however, pine wood is a worthy sub and you will see why momentarily.

Sapphire paint, a gold earring and necklace, these items can also be silver; maybe some jewelry you don't use any more, costume jewelry can sub as well.

The Way of the Warlock

The wishbone of a dove or a turkey's wishbone will suffice; we are not trying to encourage you to go out and kill a dove or a turkey for its wishbone because this would be in the realm of stereotypical [black magic] witchcraft. You can also buy a whole chicken from the grocery store. They are cheap and you can even use its wishbone as a worthy substitute.

Olive or almond oil if you cannot find original olive or almond wood.

When it comes to the rod, a perfect rod would be a drumstick since they are around the same size and taper off at the tip.

First, carve a groove somewhat in the middle of the rod just long enough for the single end of the wishbone to be fitted in.

If you don't have the required type of wood, take the rod that you do have, get a small paint brush and completely brush over the rod with the olive or almond oil. Let it completely dry afterwards.

Next, store the rod in a high place or window to where it can be exposed to the sun's rays for a full day.

Next, get a brand new white cloth, wrap the rod securely and bury the rod in your yard for another full day. You don't have to dig a deep hole; you just want to ensure that it is covered completely with earth.

You are doing this so that the wand can absorb the powers and essence of both heaven and earth.

Once it is done, paint the rod over completely with the sapphire paint and let it dry.

After it dries, take the gold or silver necklace and wrap it around the wide end of the rod to form a grip (handle). Next, take the earring and wrap it around the neck of the tip.

Bore a small opening at the end of the tip of the rod and place the sapphire stone within the hole. You can use a dab of glue to secure the stone in the hole. Also you can use small dabs of

The Way of the Warlock

glue or small pins to keep the necklace and earring in place on the rod.

Set the wishbone in the groove with the "Y" part of the wishbone facing the tip and the single end facing the handle. You can also use a small dab of glue to secure it too.
Let the wand sit for another day. Next, recite the following incantation over the wand 3 times over: (the incantation is fully written out 3 times already so that you won't lose your place).

I hereby declare this wand to be
A viable conduit of spiritual power through me
I hereby declare this wand to be
A viable conduit of spiritual power through me
I hereby declare this wand to be
A viable conduit of spiritual power through me
Whatever I wish
Whatever I decree
The blessing returns
Fully in tact to me
Whatever I wish
Whatever I decree
The blessing returns
Fully in tact to me
Whatever I wish

Whatever I decree
The blessing returns
Fully in tact to me

I hereby declare this wand to be
A viable conduit of spiritual power through
me
I hereby declare this wand to be
A viable conduit of spiritual power through
me
I hereby declare this wand to be
A viable conduit of spiritual power through
me
Whatever I wish
Whatever I decree
The blessing returns
Fully in tact to me
Whatever I wish
Whatever I decree
The blessing returns
Fully in tact to me
Whatever I wish
Whatever I decree
The blessing returns
Fully in tact to me

I hereby declare this wand to be
A viable conduit of spiritual power through
me
I hereby declare this wand to be
A viable conduit of spiritual power through
me
I hereby declare this wand to be

The Way of the Warlock

A viable conduit of spiritual power through
me
Whatever I wish
Whatever I decree
The blessing returns
Fully in tact to me
Whatever I wish
Whatever I decree
The blessing returns
Fully in tact to me
Whatever I wish
Whatever I decree
The blessing returns
Fully in tact to me

Let it sit for one more day; now the
wand is ready to use. Use it as follows:
stand in a window or outside. Point the
wand towards the sky. Whatever it is
that you are wanting to obtain, see it in
your mind's eye. Next, see the image in
your mind transform to a bright white
light. Imagine that light traveling from
your mind, through your neck, and
shoulder, down your arm and entering
the wand from your hand through the
handle. Next, see the light shooting into
the sky in the form of a white laser
beam. See the laser beam as touching
the sky and causing a colossal sized
image of what you want on the huge sky
screen. See the huge image on the sky

turn into the brilliant white light again and come back to you; imagine the "V" part of the wishbone catches the light and see the light traveling back into the wand, through your hand and arm, back up into your mind. Finally, utter the words:

"Let it be so."

Chapter 5: Lucidity (The Clear Mind)

Lucidity is the way of the warlock; it is being fully conscious to experience life wholly (Holy) and be in a prime position to recognize and receive all the blessings that it has to offer; lucidity is nothing more than having a clear mind. Lucidity is clarity and clarity is power unimpeded. A clear mind is needed. There is a saying that "cleanliness is next to Godliness;" most don't take into consideration the deeper meaning of this cliché. Many think of having a clean house or car and mistakenly attribute this (outward cleanliness) to being Godlike. If only I had a nickel for the number of outwardly clean lunatics that I've encountered. That's right; the truth of the matter is that some of the most evil people to ever walk the planet have been neat freaks or outwardly clean and organized as a matter of (mechanical) habit. Many of them present this persona simply because they are so "messy" (if you will) on the inside. And it is a ploy to sway you. Therefore, this proverb must have a much deeper and richer inner meaning. This "saying" is talking about clarity of mind: mental cleanliness because God Himself dwells in a clear or clean mind. If a clean physical house was all it took then every church known to man would be filled with the proverbial "Glory of the Lord." Your mental household is what needs to be cleaned up so that God can make His abode there. Once this happens, your power and acumen will know absolutely no boundaries.

To be lucid is to be completely rational. It means to have a clear mind and emit (spiritual) light. It is the "light" itself that works the magic. Perhaps the number one issue with the so-called spiritually in tuned ones that attempt to help others is their lack of lucidity. Their minds are like radios with the dial caught between two different stations: both stations are attempting to dominate the airwaves and all that is heard is a cluster of confused noise, nonsense, and static. This is the mental state of the average human being. This mental static only serves to hinder the magical results you seek. Lucidity, the clear mind, is the way to freedom and power. Visualization and incantations (words) can only do so much. The words and mental imageries

The Way of the Warlock

need the spiritual juice (the power) to go out and accomplish that which they are designed to do.

The following is a spiritual exercise that is purposely designed to start the process of cleaning up the mind. It should be done everyday for at least 5 to 10 minutes for starters. You will want to gradually get to the point to where you are doing it at least 30 minutes a day. The exercise is called…

Present Time Imagery

Sit in a quite room in a comfortable chair. The palms of your hands should be face down on your lap. Take about 2 to 3 minutes to get a good gander at the room you are in; carefully look at and consider as much as you can; next close your eyes and visualize the room exactly as you remember it. Do your best to make the image as vivid as possible and hold the image as long as you can. Try to keep this up for at least 5 minutes at first.

Visualization can be a cumbersome process for many because of a cloudy and static filled mindset. Many people even think that they can't visualize, but this is not the case; they are just victims of another faulty mindset. Faithful practice of this exercise will begin the process of clearing your mental atmosphere. It is imperative that you do not get discouraged. Even if the only thing you can see in your mind's eye is a vague image of the coffee table in front of you, hold that image as long as possible. Over time the image will clear up and other images will follow suit and appear within the image, perhaps an end table or picture on the wall will pop into your head. Gradually the picture will continue to build upon itself until you have the entire room within your mental scope; finally, you yourself will appear in the picture; your visualization, concentration, and focusing skills will be getting stronger and acquiring more spiritual and mental power. As your focus and concentration increases, distractions decrease, and at last, you will be creating for yourself that miraculous life that you once thought impossible so again I say be diligent and don't give up.

Stop the Madness & Design Your Life (Spiritual Exercises)

Stop the Madness

The following spiritual exercise is called "stop the madness." With it, you can initiate the process of designing your life exactly the way you want it to be by the way of the warlock; to design your life, all you have to do is master your words, be careful how you used them, and be sure to not use them against yourself. Negative verbalizations will sabotage your efforts. Initially, negative thoughts will come to you. You won't be able to stop them at first; however, you can totally control your tongue if you focus hard enough. Negative energy will bombard your mind and conjure up negative and hurtful mental monologues, dialogues, scenes, and images. Your job is to simply watch them come and go. Watch but don't act them out. By doing this (refusing to speak or act out on the negativity), you are sending your mind a very powerful message. You are stopping the madness and telling it that you don't want to operate like that anymore. Yes,

you want to cease with the insanity.
Your mind will eventually get it, put on
the brakes, and do an about-face in the
other direction. Practice this everyday all
day. Do not attempt or struggle with
trying to be positive. The negativity that
you experience is an auto-response
process. Positivity should flow (naturally
& effortlessly) in the same manner. So
don't worry about trying to be positive.
Just refuse to be obedient to the
negative nature and positive spiritual
power will come to you. This is one of
your daily spiritual exercises. It can be
done at anytime of day or night for an
indefinite period of time, so be sure and
do it.

Design Your Life

Here is a supplemental spiritual exercise. Start on a Monday and end on a Sunday; faithfully do these exercises one week out of the month for the whole year. Do one a day. It will only take about 5 minutes a day. You can do it for longer if you like; it wouldn't hurt at all. You can even reinforce it by doing it two weeks out of a month or everyday if you like or have time, but one week out of the month will suffice if you have a very busy schedule. Below is a recap of the previous list from Chapter 2, "The Power of Words." Notice that there are seven items on the list. This is by intentional design. There is one item for each day of the week; read over the list:

Monday: Virtually fearless mind

Tuesday: Riches and wealth (more than you could ever hope to spend in your lifetime).

Wednesday: Correct and erase past errors [not repeating mistakes over and over again, by releasing bad and negative attitudes].

Thursday: Robust vigorous health, vitality, and unlimited energy

Friday: True love and healthy relationships

Saturday: Cast away demons that vex you and employ angels to minister unto you

Sunday: True (real) conscious relationship with the Creator of all things seen and unseen beyond your current imaginary relationship (above intellectual knowing).

Let's start with…

Monday

What would it mean to you if you were completely fearless? Be realistic. We are not talking about gung-ho arrogant foolishness, being conceited and cocky, nor are talking about prideful states and other foolish nonsense. We are not talking about the fear that is commonly mistaken for spiritual intelligence either. This is for the purpose of "self preservation." It truly isn't fear at all; it is angelic intelligence and power that stems from God working on your behalf. For instance, if you attempt to cross a busy street and suddenly a car barrels down upon you, that overwhelming urge which causes you to leap out of the way for safety is actually divine intelligence intervening on your behalf. It is not fear. Fear is a demonic force. It is the demonic forces that concern us here.

We are talking about irrational fear: the anxiety you feel around other people, in crowded areas, or in enclosed spaces, the depressed states you go through day in and day out, that vague sense of melancholy that hovers at the surface of your mind but you really can't quite understand what it's all about, the

The Way of the Warlock

incessant frustration that hounds you because other (inconsiderate or independent) people won't behave or act in ways that pleases you, feelings of dismay and discouragement because circumstances and events are not panning out the way you believe they should, states of loneliness that make you long for the "good ol' days" of the past. Uncertainty about the future for yourself and other loved ones can be added to the list, and what about full blown phobias or post traumatic stresses that rob you of your ability to fully experience and engage in life. This is the kind of fear that we are talking about. So go for it and imagine…

What if you had not one single irrational fear? How would your life be different? What would you be doing differently about your current circumstances?

You are not being charged to take action in the physical world but in the mental world that governs the physical. Just imagine what your life would be like; do it for about 5 minutes; get up and go on about your business and forget about the exercise; this is all you need to do. You are to do the very same

The Way of the Warlock

thing for the other days; ask yourself the same questions that pertain to each day's consideration and visualize what your life would be like, so let's move on to…

Tuesday

What if you had more riches and wealth than you could ever hope to use or spend in your life? How would your life be different? What would you be doing differently about your current circumstances?

Wednesday

What if you could correct and erase all past errors [not repeating mistakes over and over again, by releasing bad and negative attitudes]. How would your life be different? What would you be doing differently about your current circumstances?

Thursday

What if you had total robust vigorous health, vitality, and unlimited energy? How would your life be different?

The Way of the Warlock

What would you be doing differently about your current circumstances?

Friday

What if you had true love and healthy relationships?
How would your life be different?
What would you be doing differently about your current circumstances?

Saturday

What if you could [permanently] cast away demons that vex you and employ angels to minister unto you? How would your life be different? What would you be doing differently about your current circumstances?

Sunday

What if you had a true (real) conscious relationship with the Creator of all things seen and unseen beyond your current imaginary relationship (above intellectual knowing). What if [like Christ] you were one with God? How would your life be different? What would you be doing differently about your current circumstances?

The Way of the Warlock

It really is possible to design your life exactly the way you want it to be. Be diligent and faithful with these exercises. And magic will definitely happen. You will experience the magic of a transformed nature of spiritual freedom.

Conclusion

That last statement you just read was meant to be a hint. The real underlying purpose of this book is that of inner magic. That's right: the inner magic of a transformed nature. The bible calls it the "renewing of the mind." This is what the real magic is all about. Renewing the mind cultivates real faith and with true faith, the outer (worldly) magic is made completely possible, so go ahead and do the spells, rituals, and incantations as it pleases you, but if you don't do anything else, be sure to practice the exercises "stop the madness," "design your life," along with the "present time imagery," and "catching the lies" as noted in chapter two, and let the magic take place.

God Bless

Points to Ponder

1. God did not create religion. Man did.

2. Religion was created in a vain attempt to understand why we come and go.

3. What is life about? This question shouldn't be asked. Asking it has driven many people insane.

4. The statement, "I know the Lord," is the first of all religious taboos that paves the way to all the others.

5. All is not lost; a brainwashed individual can be brain-cleansed.

6. "What is my personal life supposed to be about," is the better question.

7. You cannot know God, but you can connect to Him.

8. Only God is capable of true healing.

The Way of the Warlock

9. Witches prolong their lives by tricking others into being ensnared by the devil.

10. The way of the witch is not the way of the warlock.

11. Warlocks have been cleverly concealed within the ranks of the church.

12. These warlocks (within the clergy) are very crafty in that they can steal souls immediately.

13. Many (women accused of being) witches were tortured and executed in an effort to drive away the devil.

14. The witches were "sacrificial lambs" condemned by the hypocritical warlocks to throw the church congregations off their very own devilish scents.

15. Unlike the stereotypical hypocrite, a real warlock is a man of God that has the power to heal and edify.

The Way of the Warlock

16. The warlock's goal is that of mental freedom and spiritual awakening.

17. People are going bananas and losing faith because of negativity swimming around in their heads.

18. Misapplied words is what jumpstarted the negative mindsets.

19. People are either rising or falling (mentally, physically, and spiritually) because of words.

20. If you don't have that same delightful sense of well being and cheeriness you once had as a child, then you have been misapplying your words and could be headed in the wrong direction.

21. The power of words can literally change your life for the better practically overnight.

22. You must first realize where you are; you can then grow from there.

The Way of the Warlock

23. Words contain power because people invest emotional energy into them.

24. The "way of the warlock" can make you a master of words; hence you become a master of life.

25. Realization equals implementation. This is a spiritual law.

26. You may have used words to render yourself powerless by fostering "intellectual knowing."

27. It's time to stop using your words to tell yourself lies. You can disengage from lying to yourself.

28. You really don't trust God; if you did, then all would be well.

29. Watch how you misapply your words to pull the rug from out under your feet.

30. You have to gain control of your words; other people, situations,

and circumstances are
irrelevant.

31. You have used the power of your
words to create an alternate
(mental) world that clouds over
and sometimes completely
overshadows or veils the real
world that you must deal with.
Just about every other person on
the planet has done exactly the
same thing.

32. You fear the real world because it
does not match the inner
imaginary world that you've
created.

33. By using words to create the
imaginary world, you have
shunned the Creator.

34. You must get in touch with the
person (your real inner self) that
used the power of words to talk
your mind into that neurotic state
that now creates and shapes
your outer world of people,
relations, and circumstances.

The Way of the Warlock

35. Even physical illnesses you may be struggling with happened because you used the power of your words against yourself.

36. The Egyptians used the power of words to influence the spiritual essence behind all things physical (not just other human beings) and just like people, every thing else in the environment responded.

37. Incantations, invocations, and certain rituals that include spells and usage of symbols all involved words that supposedly had power instilled within to influence the Creator much in the same way we use them to influence other people.

38. Moses, who was raised in Egypt, understood "world bending" completely when he told the Israelites, "Stand still, and behold the salvation of the Lord!"

39. "Air bending" at its finest was demonstrated when Christ Himself uttered the infamous, "Peace, be still!" and calmed the storm.

40. Matter is mind condensed into solid form.

41. Fear is the sole reason for the invention of religion.

42. Man fears he cannot control his life so he uses religion to foster (illusory) control of life by controlling other people. He does not know God so he attempts to be a god.

43. We are taught to not covet money (by the clergy); however, the church is always hungrily seeking after money.

44. You were meant to have more than enough money to live a content and comfortable life.

45. Please be mindful of your very own behavioral tendencies.

The Way of the Warlock

46. We are spiritual creatures enclosed in physical vessels. Spells and incantations bridge the gap between the spirit and matter.

47. Spells work by way of the "power of suggestion" because an individual is incapable of properly and consistently guarding his mind.

48. Lucidity is the way of the warlock; it is being fully conscious to experience life wholly (Holy) and be in a prime position to recognize and receive all the blessings that it has to offer; it means to have a clear mind, and clarity is power unimpeded.

49. It really is possible to design your life exactly the way you want it to be. Be diligent, faithful, and magic will definitely happen.

50. With the proper usage of words, you will experience the magic of a transformed life of happiness and continuous blessings by way of your new spiritual nature.

The Way of the Warlock

THE END

The Way of the Warlock

More Books by the Author
Available at Amazon books

The Power of Spiritology, Book I

The Power of Spiritology, Book II, I Am the Devil

The Power of Spiritology, Book III, Let Go Your Ego

The Power of Spiritology, Book IV, Exercises For Spiritual Growth & Mind Renewal

PsychoSpiritual Awareness, The Way of Spiritual Evolution

PsychoSpiritual Awareness II: Reclaim your Fearless Self

PsychoSpiritual Awareness III, Guide For The Shy Guy: How to Have Confidence with Women

The Power of Alchemy, The Higher Science of God

The Power of Alchemy II, The Higher Religion of God

The Truth About Prayer: Every Thought a Prayer

The Way of the Warlock

The Way of the Warlock

Proof

Made in the USA
Charleston, SC
05 February 2016